The Mirror Chronicles

by Marc Darnell

ISBN: 978-81-19654-21-5

First Edition: 2024
Rs. 200/-

Cyberwit.net
HIG 45 Kaushambi Kunj, Kalindipuram
Allahabad - 211011 (U.P.) India
http://www.cyberwit.net
Tel: +(91) 9415091004
E-mail: info@cyberwit.net

for my parents

Donald and Mary

Contents

The 2nd Second Coming

Another beast is loosed upon a dozing earth—
a thing with fanged veneers slouches toward the nations
as fields fill with vitamin rain and hormone rations
permeating the cloned calves now veal at birth.
The troposphere is coughing out medicinal meth
while fetuses make early crib death reservations,
although the dopest obstetricians are on vacation—
Abilify just makes them sadly less depressed.
Over-sexted phones are filling up the oceans
as well as bitter former floes that just aren't cool.
The sleeker on-sale beasts that came before were vices—
a Siri laughing, announcing you're an organic tool,
and ergonomic chairs stained with quick-dry drool
from troglodytes turned on by sex-changing devices.

Aerie

Up somewhere
they fondle their eggs, slick-downy cool
and nouveau normal, endorsing their
peaceful mob rule—

these proper birds roosting
in 2.5 bathroom nests to spot a chicken who never
perches the way they do, cooing
in tongues with their secret talon-shakes, clever

in their rippleless swan dives beneath
the chicken's dignity, bad at disguising
their envy that it's clucking unique,
so I say *pluck these fat faux cocks*, eulogizing

the earthbound dodo, and squawk at all
bullying— a suet bar of birdseed bull.

Blushless

He'd stay a boy,
forever innocent, with adolescence
frozen— no erotic joys
nor sexual prominence

to flaunt around— the easy explanation:
biology wasn't very kind,
depriving him of testosterone, of hair's invasion,
a man maturing missing in his mind,

going through years of purest thinking—
no pulsing flesh or slight protrusion,
free of testicular outbursts, yet gazing
at bodies barely clothed with sad confusion,

no liberation from the chains of naivety—
a trait innate at his nativity.

Abandonado

Where is everybody?
Tell us where they are—
moved on and left us behind?

Some were the bullying kind,
often far
into the heads of everybody

else, always giddy
to find a weak one to scar
till he cowered behind

others with weaker minds,
who were also sick with fear.
Where is everybody

who said they were ready
to defend us— to listen, not hear?
But they've flown, left us behind

and earthbound to never find
a heaven anywhere.
Who thought everybody
would leave the lonely behind?

The Mirror Chronicles 1

To stay a catch and keep a tight resilience,
I calmed my face— no extra ecstasy
or look of awe or horror, no pestilence
of smiles— thinking idiotically

that living crevice-free is nine-tenths
of all that really floats, but now I dive
towards a state of cracking convalescence,
old libido flaked and unalive.

We timid, runted boys have never fared
too well in wars waged by the handsomest,
the tallest, the most robust, the least scarred,
and I'm unclear of the rightful place of just

homely looks and above-average wit—
so much coveted is full of shit.

The Mirror Chronicles 2

Decide tonight to stop— leave every wound
sutured— no more bruising like a bard
bouncing bad decisions in your mind
susceptible to dipping fits but hard

to classify deranged, an intellect
fragile from the start. Tell your heart
it's time to show its mercy, stop attacks
upon itself that make you always hurt.

Don't resort to thoughts of bang and bleed
or act as though you've never had a mentor—
we're all casualties, lost in needs.
Arise, you're not the world's woeful center,

and no one wants to hear your fixed lamenting—
perhaps your suffering's motives need amending.

The Mirror Chronicles 3

How do you love me, have you counted the ways?
Is it my red Rasputin beard that holds
you captive, the bags beneath my bloodshot eyes?
Could it be my papa belly that holds

undesirable viruses, E. coli
revved to spread infection. I am told
my teeth protrude and I am not that wise.
My hair falls out, my hands are always cold.

How do I love myself is more the question–
where is my heart once large, where is the passion
I felt at twenty? Now I live a prison
atrophying, dying is a mission.

How do I love *you*– stranger in the mirror?
I keep it dark, the truth in light I fear.

Char Man

This room is orange, its walls are hot,
I'm trapped within a molten mint,
the brittle floor a crimson tint,
the roof, stalactites drying out—

this is the cave I live, what brought
me here— a darkly moral slant—
a guilty thug, an anti-saint
rising as a fly from rot.

I eat myself, the food of hell.
With brimstone veins, my soul flew
to find a child to beat within.

I'm sere, no sweat or blood to spill
upon this plane of magma flow,
circling round my vat of sins.

Enigmatic Poet

It's okay to talk mysteriously.
You'd love to confess
your sins, the dirtiest,
but you're the best censor
to your filth and childishness.

It isn't always straightforwardness
that makes a poem beautifully burn.
Life is more perplexing every day—
you don't have to clarify
or illustrate the wheels that turn.

Yet try time to time not to amaze,
but leave a message, a crystal mark,
before you've wandered your words,

though you've always run us through a maze
while you connive in the dark,
riding a rift that only widens.

Colossus Of Rhodes

Bless the muscles of those
chiseling your colossus
and those erecting it,
dear blinding Helios.
They require no armies,
only dumber species
dragging your pieces for miles,
and certainly will christen it
a hulk of flattery,
devout idolatry,
propped on a pedestal,
gored in latest Greek.
You like how they are weak
but not that they are weary
of gods with human lust.
Instead you're mortified
you're losing ground as deity
and yearn to know the odds,
the fate of multiple gods.
Though they break your bust
and limbs from hardest quarries,
eventually they'll turn
to one and only one.
A loner god will rise
erasing all the rest,
adored but left alone.
Who knows how long he'll last?
The needs of mortals shift,
so cherish the reign that's left.

You'll be dismembered long
before the shaking earth
sinks you in the sea.
It's time to cut your losses
and rest your chariot
to water your melting horses.

Da Prezadent

The orange king with yellow hair
is leaping up and down again
and says he has no clothes to wear.

Nothing fits, and people stare
but won't go in this lion's den—
the orange king with yellow hair

who picks a fight and has to share
the land with rather smarter men
and says he has no clothes to wear

on really big occasions where
he boasts his brain and then offends
the masses till they tear their hair

and wonder where there children are,
if they are ousted citizens
who soon might have no clothes to wear

if he rubs out Obamacare
and poverty is *great again.*
The orange king with yellow hair
is crying in his underwear.

Community Service

He thinks of blonder days to kill the sting
of sweeping city streets he used to own,
when he paid highest price for new faux things—
some thought he owned a portion of the moon.

A bully bred, he also had the looks—
Casanova delts and hair to spare.
He raised his brow making homeless jokes
and tried to charge a fee to share his air.

He sent his wife adrift, then searched the fold,
celebrated drunk and killed a fence.
In jail, the new fluff fleeced him, took his gold
then fluffed him off— she found a newer prince.

Now he stabs the trash, each car that passes
asks him where the cheapest tank of gas is.

Cruel Lens

Quickly she'd risen
to be a screen star
of nouveau wonder
in a marquee prison

of rouged illusions
where tantrums were
made mediocre
with drugs' infusions.

Fame's short stint
was weaned by looks
pruned and tuned,

last years spent—
a wrinkle who evoked
pathos to the end.

December Lights

'Tis the season lights begin their reign
to roost upon the eaves of every home.
To us they were the colors of our pain
and beacons of our uninvited fears,
our father's acts and their resulting tears.

Crimson was his urge to conquer flesh—
our innocence became a thing to snuff,
coming to our open rooms with Mom
asleep, or so we thought, we were the stuff
adoption bought, and so much better fresh.

The green was deep when looking in his eyes,
a force that drained and wove a loneliness
forever in our lives, and azure was
the hope that we held onto in the sky—
it's where we went each time he whispered *close
your eyes.* We'd put on extra layers of clothes
to stretch the time before he reached our thighs.

As ambiance in nightmares that remain,
violet gives the devil's guided tour
where he we loathed perfected every lure
before the pretty lights came on again.

Gift Card

What to give to those who have it all—
the well-to-do will scoff your gift of roses.
They must own an Eden one supposes
of Van Gogh irises so proud and tall,

and every night these gluttons crash the ball
with fashion contraband and skyward noses
(when paupers speak the rich make animal noises).
Platinum paying— they covet no cash at all

and eat their young before the feds attack.
Plastic is taboo on their estates—
the dirty poor— they opt for imitation.

Prognosis of their airs is not exact,
depending on the heirs they choose as mates,
fear of losing all no limitation.

Defibrillate

Wounds to heart don’t bleed—
they prevent us from turning to stone.
Pain shakes up what’s near dead.

Can even soul’s oldest gangrenes
revive the body in that pissed-up bed
amidst the Stonehenge of machines?

The Gardener

All hail Albert Gardner
who protects the sanctum of his century plant,
exposing it to moonlight and music
as the night reveals hints of a storm
he can't yet comprehend, due to his senility.
His slowly uprooting, blue-green veins

jiggle as he tills the soil, veins
barked and stalked to the heart of the gardener,
healthy for his age despite his senility
which can make him forget he owns a century plant.
Rain now begins, but he has no sense of storm
as he goes inside to put on more music,

thinking green things thrive from greener music—
Bach now, wisping the chlorophyll in their veins
like the wind circulates the storm
still unnoticed by the gardener
wondering what year of this century, plant
in bloom, he'll be botanically hallmarked (senility

at bay, hopefully) a champion. It is senility
encroaching his world, leaving a cramped space of music
and this nurtured idol of his century (plants
love adoration), needing no rain in its veins—
hardier than cacti in Albert's garden, or
pseudo-Eden, Eve-less, storm-

less for the moment, but a storm
is a storm, and soon fractures his shell of senility,
the torrent, without mercy, uprooting all in his garden, or
drowning it in rain, a power outage cutting the music,
stilling the too viscous blood in Albert's veins.
When the lightning finally passes only the century plant

remains, but trauma has taken the century plant's
bud, now gone. He pulls it up, his fogged storm
of confusion lifting momentarily, ridding his veins
of a life of bewilderments, jarring that grip of senility
as electricity reconnects his severed music.
But he wants no longer to be a perennial gardener

but a gardener of finite annuals, to finally end his century— plant
things with mortality, like him, to Mozart's Nachtmusik, accepting
the storm
of gentle senility— that vine of comfort through the final years of
his veins.

Habitual Victim

Knowing he'd be saved, he tried to drown— we thought
he was screaming for help, but only waving and yawning.
He chewed attention raw— a wolf licking and gnawing
his favorite catastrophes, for him such comfortable spots.
To know him was to know he'd want a close-range shot
that missed the major parts of his brain as long as pain
was good and hard and brought gut and glory. When cain
was raised to tingling hairy heights, the shock-monger ate
compassion, but looking for abuse can lead to ruin
(woe is he without a wowed and oohing audience).
Our eyes grew tired of his forced blood and broken bones,
recurring slits and scabbings of little or no substance,
till one day he cried wolf, though wolf left him alone:
we chose a tree, he hanged till dead with our assistance.

Licker License

I am tongue, conductor of taste,
who whips out words from that throaty fathom—
I give them souls then cast
them out to the air, that fat medium

of noise. I am human
snake who can fabricate or tell a
truth that fosters deep love when
I use sexy sibilance the

lonely wait for. I taste the sour of color
across the room before the eyes see it.
I hate the eyes, that they assume oracular
is everything— I hate their quiet

overhead governance of me, of the room,
but I can't escape this tonsil tomb.

Magnetism

Do you feel the pull, the sway,
even when I'm far away?
That's the reach of our attraction,
the reign of two sure hearts.
Many have a fragile union
and fail to fit— the gift of hurt
their only thing to offer,

but you're this body's only lover.
I lack, you being so far,
but distance isn't the culprit
in our bond, but time apart.
We can do nothing about it.
And time was never my favorite unit of measure,
but level of our love and all its pleasures.

Neighborhood Watch

Some say it doesn't qualify
to say our love is ample proof
we're meant to be. It fortifies
that we are bonded and aloof,
and I won't quit till we unlove,
unravel from their alienation.
To turn away is nothing shy of
brave, ignoring their abrasions.
I've never understood intrusion—
it's never been their business, we
can build a bigger fence, live on
less, and we don't have to be
pillars of this community
or fit their frame of family.

"Passing" Thoughts

I will fall so freely (forever would be fine),
holding on to no one into the cleanest gulf
of dark matter— that's heaven, it's what you can't see,
and, though it will be no valley, I'll fear no evil—
at least in theory. Those who sought my bones in life
may find a different falling, a hotter one. I
was always afraid to skydive, afraid I'd pull the cord
too late— like I'd live if I did, hope not, a rubber
vomit splat in bed. One can fall to heaven,
right? There's no direction in the afterlife.
The before and after thing will be as simple as
a bubble breaks— here to there no in between
of toil, pain— no burning or stinging to tear away
what once were eyes, assuming I go to the good place. I
was good, right? I'm sure I hurt more than a few
people, caused one or two suicides or addictions.
Well they caused a few of mine. I think death
is fair— no promise of ascension or deistic
enterprise. No prophet proved that (G)(g)od(s) exist,
but wow, what stories— burning bush— acid trip?
We trust too many mouths that trusted others before.
I'm sure the whatever-after, the ever-laughter after,
is magical, and horrific. Fear the so-so unknown—
it's human. It's called ignorance. I will fall
so freely, off the earth, if I die in Australia.
Wait, I forgot in death there's no gravity.

Conflagrate

Let your outside die— it's not
surrender, but self-preservation: the dead

parts need to finish their rot.
Let new skin take the lead

into the wilderness of familiar pains
and pierce that old charcoal shield.

Protect your inner, firstborn veins,
your secret seed

that tells you who you are each morning in bed.
Callused vessel of decay— we feed

you to the sun, the world, the nearest burning field.

The Lottery*

The ones I left behind desired my leaving
Long before, their yearly feting fruitful—
Immolation prime but thick with grieving,
Familial betrayal my removal,

With democratic, mob rule approval.
Each participant said, "He who's drawn
Must give," then drew it down to me— a jovial,
Lyrical, front-line loser. I was drawn

To souls of hope, to each one's brutal stone,
Its heart-felt hesitation, but still elective.
As savior, allow me a regal moment dethroned,
I pled, but no, and I bled on, a thing of

Sick signification, who played the wheel
That flattens lives, and gaily slips the rail.

*1948 short story by Shirley Jackson

tock

time like a diamond
like a crystal clock
you shine with the soberest face
one central eye two brutal hands
that wear the soul down
without a trace

you beat the man in the field
who hurries and worries with the last day clouds
counting the drowned and the burned-up yield
his siren wife in his head so loud

and tease the broken woman
in a bed of white
strapped in a skin so tight
she cries for the midnight
but the fluorescent light
stays on

1st poem, age 13

Two-Legged

Pain from walking upright
bothers him all night—
the curse of bipedal man
evolved to more than trite
quadrupedal scum.

He's perpendicular
to soup he slithered from—
those eras he was just
a bald amphibian.

Each time he tries to rest,
he still feels the cruel
pangs his spine amassed
during its pivot and duel
with earth's daily pull.

It's hard for human hearts
to pump in upright bodies—
up and down blood goes,
a platelet waterfall
to brains and grounded veins.

He asks *What's next for men—*
no legs at all, and then?
clutching a knot in his chest.

This time it doesn't leave.
He'll never know, as friends
stand slumped beside his grave.

Woe Is He

To write depressing thoughts can be an art
if the author emphasizes pain—
see the manic crying from the rain
who scribbles that he feels worlds apart

and then becomes a hero from his scars,
cataloged and pickled up with praise—
his sobs in ink are epic, more than stains.
Some are quick to praise him from the start,

wrinkles in his reasoning ignored
(how sad for sane soliloquies unsaid).
And when in death his genius expires,

his unseen expertise much more adored,
convinced he was sincere but very sad,
they deck his grave and cry beside the pyre.

All Hallows'

O rabid eve of dark and bone and witch
and other iconography we spin,
hot with cancered coil, newt and stitch,
fly my hagged broom into the wind.

I crave my black-on-amber silhouette
accompanied by one ripe crack of thunder.
Unholiest of ghosts, knight me the bat
that spits the air and awes the young with wonder—

this month of moans, the only span I see
unbiblical bombastic plastic gore,
a haunted heart a possibility,
and slimed tales that end *forevermore,*

when evil's mocked but never understood,
and needled sweets diffuse the neighborhood.

assistance requested in junior misses

makeup mirrors
and dagger heels
abound here,
and saccharine aisles
churn with hired
hags, with hills
of alien pastel
hair dyes to steal
a piece of paragon,
as pseudo-virgins dab on
caked and runny
lodes of hormonal appeal

glossy-lipped, sunny
dispositions rule,
and if you find it odd
the homage that's paid
to pink and pinking,
this menstrual pastorale
holds no serenity
for you, with eau de
overkill stinking,
sinking
beneath size zero
to the clearance tag below

astral travel

I stay
when my
body leaves
the house

it moves
moves moves
while I
perch in
my chair
coughing stanzas

when I
drive the
web of
the city
my soul
stays in
bed embracing
lover ghosts

distance from
my body
is survival
till the
day it's
in the
ground and
I remain
confused above
it forever

Banana On The 12th Floor

No matter the day,
no matter if I rise with a love-cancered heart,
if I dreamed of falling and wanting it,
if I embraced another past lust-ghost,
if I am sloth and good liar, good fabricator,
if I beg to evaporate,
no matter my godless life,

I'll eat a banana by the window
when I churn with acid regrets—
to continue as a hole that consumes
potassium oh conqueror of cramps,
who sucks it up like a good buttercup
the phrase *life is too short!*
and pretends to revel that the chest beats—
that heart that holds me hostage to living.
I hate bananas.

grr

it was in the woods
there's always a thing in the woods
wherever you live a woods isn't a woods
unless a hairy pseudo-sapien builds a nest
deep in and not like a bird's nest
a bedbug heap of leper sticks the woods
rejected too freak for dainty nests

so they knew a thing was in the woods
a lurch-happy quasimodo making a nest
that it wanted to do four things
guard its hepatitis a b and c cootie nest
make dung that rivaled the dung of death
eat pets cattle but not be well-photographed
and never eat people but gash them to death

it went growly on deer who tripped on things
rocks bumps of dirt and decayed things
it killed long before its human deaths
but then a city girl caught it shitting photographed
it and tripped on a rock was scratched to death
by this enigmatic romantic folklore thing

kids found the camera developed the photograph
showed a teacher who showed the sheriff
they weren't lovers but wanted to have a thing
now everyone knew something was in the woods
felt they fit in because other woods

by other towns had something in the woods
rumors fads raves come and go it was the thing

everyone lock your doors by six said the sheriff
they heard snaps and grrs in the woods
consoling their tykes that monsters didn't exist
but everyone was giddy they did exist
like halloween forever till they found the sheriff
decapitated surprise! in a jockstrap by the woods

but that's still like halloween then the sheriff's
body vanished zombie? wrong genre hairballs
were found nearby lycan? wrong genre the sheriff's
head was found on a stick at the edge of the woods
deliverance hillbilly hell? wrong genre the woods
were droll disappointing so now the thing
was in town where it would try to exist
instead of in the woods as a nostalgic thing

it would be a board-elected hairball
maybe shave buy a house or cabin in the woods
but not pay taxes since it was cryptozoic didn't exist
they'd find in diners bathrooms bars its hairballs
when they saw it they'd treat it like a hairball
so shit sick of it diss it like it didn't exist

blow out your candles

my wish this year is all
at once we be pulled
into the sky as a spoiled
ball of whine be shot to the
sun but that means planes
drop out of the sky and car
pile-ups become oxidized
snakes and zoo prisoners
slowly starve trees about
to be felled in minutes
drop later on innocent
fawns roses about to be
watered go thirsty till the
next rain and that could
be months in Nebraska
where cattle escape now
called the Encroaching
Grass State and drywall
cities return to muck
and saltpeter but nuke goo
would leak from missiles
power plants crack with
mustard fog and despite the
radioactive seeping and
starving of domesticated
beasts who can't plant crops
big booms unsupervised
dams shit-up sewers earth
still recovers or vomits it

we'd be an abundance of
protein to fauna and fossil
fuels have unnamed geologic
eras to replenish before
something evolves maybe
with scales this time to
fuck it up again round 2

doubt

is a ghost in his mind
that talks him

out of
acting on true love

he thought it a friend
shielding him from

the perils of bravery—
that sparse piece of sky

where the lonely fly and hunt
and the caverns where too much love

might leave him weak
or grief turn him gaunt

he hopes by next week
it finds another wimp to haunt

email response after my suggestion to read
"Thirteen Ways Of Looking At A Blackbird"
by Wallace Stevens

I'll

have you know

I

spent 35 years

teaching writing

and

literature

at various colleges and

universities and

before that

got

a PhD in lit

at UC Irvine so I

know that
poem very
well thank you

Horizontal/Vertical Sonnet

Where I've taken my heart, the way I've bled,
Is what I write about, and when in pain,
The heart is what I blame and distrust, but the
Heart is a muscle, thrust and pumper first,
Now until the tender blood goes hard,
In sync with body's beats, the hard breaths and urges
Our rapidly-firing, cyclic minds put us through.
Rhyme has its lovely chains, its musics bound, and I
Was one who chose its heart-like pace to contemplate.
I read my contemporaries, and often find it hard to stay
Awake through their obscure lines meant to impress
When no one's worth impressing— I learned so late
It is the soul and all its cry for clarity that some have
Left behind for inhuman lines that dwindle in my ear.

let

let the outer world slowly die
let it take your despair
let the eyes loose in the sky
let all mirrors go for a walk
with your piddly treasures
as well as the clock
the time things that measure

let what's in the ribs dance
and defy the hell of pace
let the walls be erased
and people take a bow—
they can't really get you now
let your body stand in this space
that requires no mental attendance

Over The River And Through The Woods

I

To the ones who gave me grandchildren:
you appreciated my cookies
because you saw the hearts in my eyes
as your baby teeth took the first bite,
and were grateful I gave you any damn sugar;
then you brushed and flossed after each cookie
because you knew cavities were hell cash to fix,
and we were so unfancy and destitute
we ate hot dogs with plain bread wrapped around.

You knew I needed love bounced back into me
to feel some kind of worth and purpose
for getting pregnant and not being married,
and when we eloped I didn't get a wedding dress
or even a dump cake or anything,
and when I spanked you with the wire end
of a flyswatter, you turned your head and said
yes Mommy, I will learn from spilling things;
then you skipped along to clean up the mess
and tucked yourself into bed like good gerbils.

You gave me grandchildren, because you knew
it was the least you could do, to have the same
middle-of-the-nights with crib crying for no reason.
Congratulations. I love you more.

II

To the ones who didn't give me grandchildren:
you grabbed cookies and ran,
afraid to look me in the eye
as if I had the Medusa touch, or knifing eyes.

Sterile? Is that your problem? I doubt it.
Waifish in corners, keeping to yourselves,
social caterpillars, unthankful for my love.

Sometimes I found your toothbrushes dry.
I rubbed my cracked fingers across the bristles—
cracked from scalding dishwater and clenching fists
in the cold when I didn't know where He went after work.

You're lucky I smoked outside— didn't have to—
now that's a mother, but when I swatted you
you cried, like you felt bad,
then trembled and spilled more.
Have you found your purpose yet?
Tick tock I'm in the rocker
ready to baby-cradle
one foot in the grave.
My hardship legacy ends with you I guess.
I love you less.

obituary for a bottle of beer

o golden urn
Midas kissed you into
a sunset you were
Poseidon aquarium
too sweet for demigods

you foamed like
a mad grizzly
then that barfly's
sick lipstick
mouth at you that
happy-hour cubicle bitch
spinning you down her
fuck-throat may
she still gag on
the pretzel and penis
she killed hours ago

and you go beyond
distilling in her
estrogen pit

she engulfed you
for giggles and
more sociability
on this bar stool
beside this prince
who bellied your
brothers— 4 of them

lite but they made her
look no more luscious
in his bagged eyes

but all of you
shall survive unite
in the Sewer Styx
when your souls have
been wrung through
the bowels birthed from
the bladders you
shall all come back
nectar piss purified
into the river of the reborn

obituary for an 8 x 12

longing to be a
paper airplane
creased with love
glide from an ace hand
it thought origami
was true eden

aborted from a spiral
notebook it believed
note cards were lucky
so stoic and immortal
so neon or rebel pastel

a breeze blowing it
off the table it swooped
like a barn swallow
beneath the china
cabinet where it lay
for three years

when found close to
a christmas those
sticky monkeys mutilated
it into a snowflake
now one of a kind

obituary for a PC

mercy for one
kicked from
receiving updates
dollied to the curb
2009 cubist heap

you opened the
world to us with
top 10 disasters
scabby memes
and charlie you
bit my finger

if a sin for being
too dense in
a paper-thin age
then we'll melt
you at the stake
till your keys go
Dali for cleaning
your own disk
for going beyond
the one-way scream
of the television set

forgive us with
Vista coursing
in your solder-raped

veins the oil of apes
on your tailed mouse
but garbageman Charon
won't ferry your kind

obituary for a string of lights

like a pixie crown
they lit the tree and
kept it god red
till January 1st for 3 years
giving glow to gifts
making them more
divined than they were

but as roses slowly
lose petal blood
summer by summer
so did the lights
winter by winter

allowed to bloom
two more Christmases
anemic pink
on the patchwork
wreath outside

before being coiled around
a dead sea scroll
of newspaper rot
left spent unlit beneath
the sarcophagus
of the kitchen sink

obituary for fake roses

they were good
faux folk
plucked from
their iron grid
beside vinyl windsocks
at dollar general

they spread their
arms and lips
in a vlasic pickle jar
on a lonely
janitor's table

they held their
intensity as long as
they could to
make him want to live

with their first fading
they passed as pastel
and kept slight lust
in the janitor's heart

but the sun did its due
and whitened them
though they go on
at the grave of his father

they will beautify his slab
longer than the tattered
zinnias and stitched
tulips longer than the
real blood peonies
that pray there
that die there

Lick The Plate

I eat rarely—
as punishment, duty,
for things I think are terrible about me,
so I'm at half-strength usually.

I'm a coward who lies to live,
so just an apple today.

I didn't beat shyness,
so weak, such duress,
so only liquids tomorrow.

My heart goes
on high alert, rapidly—
guiltily, around those
who watch me,

so I'll go to bed hungry
on Thursday, Friday,
so I am voluminously faded

and dream of
being sated
and bloated with love.

Beer Tastes Awful

Maybe I was driven to this—
walking 5 blocks for a 12-pack of Bud Light,
always having to piss

after 3 or 4 of them. I think I miss
a future bright
or love that feels cool like this

beer, this bliss;
then I pay for it in the morning light
with a cramped dash before I piss

my pajamas or my mattress.
In the day my chest is so tight—
maybe I was driven to this

by the absence of a kiss,
absence of love just right,
I think to myself as I take a piss.

How common to say my life is such a mess.
I should probably put up more of a fight,
but I certainly was driven to this,
to nights of emptiness and piss.

Epiphany?

Is this the moment I believe in God,
before I break and lose all sense again,
where I believe all the things It never said?

This traffic light is stuck on red
as I've come to a stop in the stagnant rain.
Is this the moment I believe in God

and find my path on this ground I plod
to a holy hut where my tears can drain
and believe all the things It never said,

hearing songs and stories read
by other sheep in constant pain?
Is this the moment I believe in God,

comforted by Its staff and rod?
A man who *hears* a god and writes it plain—
how do we know those are things it said?

How do we know It had a son that bled—
blind belief's illogical, in vain.
This is not the moment I believe in God,
where I believe all things It never said.

Help Wanted

What an absolutely sickening place to work,
so sick I can't even eat here.
People kill time, and my boss is such a jerk

the way he tells sick jokes and lurks
around and doesn't seem to care
if I have enough time to complete my work.

If you're a janitor you really talk
very little— no time, you see— and you don't wear
your heart on your sleeve or jerk

around, there's things to do, remove marks
from bathroom walls and stalls where
you see things carved in that people really had to work

at to leave there with a penknife on the stall door—
things I wouldn't doubt my boss left there—
for a good time for a good gay jerk,

hit up the new janitor, his name is Marc—
that's me. Sometimes I think I'd rather die here
than look for another hopeless place to work.
I jump from job to job I'm such a jerk.

Integrity

Sometimes you have to steal something because
you feel your job owes you,
and then you feel guilty about it later

when you're sitting at home being a people-hater.
You don't know what to do;
then you forget about it because

you're sleepy, and what was was.
The next day they know
and confront you later,

then you hear over the loudspeaker—
it's time for you to go,
pack the things on your desk because

with all the money you were given you chose
to take a piece of break room bubblegum to chew
home with you to enjoy later.

You turn off your computer,
realize everything they accused you of is true,
and you go sit in your car till 5 pm because
you're going to put back the piece of gum later.

Late Analysis

I thought things would make sense by now.
After fifty-some years I still
don't know what I'm doing.

Others look like they've been going
exactly where they want to go and will
till death, everything making sense now

by the looks on their faces, and wow,
they found ones to love and a space to fill
and act like they knew what they were doing

all along, walking working chewing,
with so much time to kill
to examine if things make sense. By now

I thought I'd be happy and life would flow,
that I'd feel rather well,
but I'm sick, not knowing what I'm doing,

and the bitter part of me hopes most are ruing
big stupid decisions and feel like hell,
that they thought things would make sense by now
and don't know what they're doing.

The Optimist

I ain't goin' nowhere,
even when I die.
There's nothing there.

You might compare
me to an atheist I
don't fit nowhere.

I sometimes scare
people who rely
on beliefs their

loved ones swear
are true about the sky,
but Nowhere

is where we always are,
we don't know why
we are here, and there

is always ache to bear—
hear this soundless cry.
I ain't goin' nowhere.
There's nothing there.

The Puffs Therapist, or Legal Drug Pusher

The Abilify isn't working?
Let's bump up the dosage.
Oh we did that last week?
Let's bump it up again, I
mean, we have to make
progress somehow. We
have you taking 19 pills
now? It's alright—the
mid 30's might be too
many. How are you?

Your speech is a little
slurred. Let me put my
sandals on the floor, and
tuck my feet under my
long, flowered, mumu-
esque long dress, it's all
the rage with therapists,
and it will be like we're
by a fire sipping white
tea, opening our hearts.

I have more free samples
of Remeron— here, chew
them up like an excellent
trooper. I have a walk-in
closet of samples, wider
than my lipstick grin.

Don't touch the tissues—
those are for people who
pay more for me, who cry
a lot and can't seem to
find themselves when
they're sitting right in
front of me— after all,
healing is a process.

You're a janitor, and you
have 2 degrees? You're
working in a very toxic
environment. You're
better than them. It's
easy to find a job in your
area. Why don't you
have a book out, silly?

You still look sad. Let's
bump something else up.
Let me get my neat wad of
notes on you. What? You
have a DUI? You're an
alcoholic. I won't see you
anymore. I'm cutting you off
suddenly from the 19 pills
I have you on. It won't be

my fault if you have the
worst nights of your life
going through the pill
withdrawals, walking in
circles for 6 hours in the

ER waiting room since it's
like restless leg syndrome
to the nth, induced by Satan.

I'm moving on, because I'm
just not getting results with
you. It's not like you're
going to have scars years
later from what I put you
through, earning your trust,
nurturing you, ditching you.

I'm billing you for the whole
hour, even though we only
talked thirteen minutes,
and you need an alcohol rehab
center. When you get there,
don't even think, mister, that
you're better than everyone.

twinge

what muscle
did I pull
when turning
to look
at you
walking away?

it is below
my shoulder blade
my could-be
wing

was I
trying to fly
and swoop you
from
your misery?

Sunflowers

Cannot help comparing
them to children,
burnt faces kissing
out to her lens.

It is September
sundown when light
is sharp and brief.
She cannot believe

they are alive
here on the edge
of death time.
She cannot remember

ever seeing her
least favorite color
this abundant, bright,
such that it

is now her favorite
for half an hour.
This is a cauldron
of yellow; it sends

eggy cries at
her photographic eyes,
photographic in that
they see everything

composed within
frames— scenes
have their white
edges where they

must stop, or,
landscapes are only
still after still.
The flowers' leaves

are tagged with green
grasshoppers
that she will
only perceive

as plentiful blurs
in picture clear.
Open shut, she
takes still after still.

Today's population
is more like a spill,
hill after hill—
the glow goes far.

She cannot conceive
their dying soon,
fending off for months
the angry sun, and

no rain, but once,
the cracked land

taking it all
for summer repairs.

Surely the insects
do not sense their
eventual starvation,
staying by the millions.

But she senses it—
the end of them
and this beautiful flow,
a flow more desperate

in this end-light than
in the power of noon.
She came to capture
a tumble of color

but freezes their
cradle pleadings,
gives them borders,
borders she will album

away with pictures
of satisfied snow.
And come tomorrow,
out of film,

she may not care
for yellow.

Never Mind

At least I'm not crazy, just sad.
What a relief. Talking about misery
turns the mad into just sad, Freud said,

but the crazies seem to have it made—
they're blaring and giddy,
may not even know the word sad.

I'd rather be dead
than talk about my pains, really,
because all the hurtful things I've said

to myself are mine only, stupid
things I've done mine to see
time and again when I'm sad

to the point I want to rid
the world of me. Common ennui
is maddening— screw what Freud said.

I'd rather be nuts instead,
backflip bat-happy,
than a man with an id incurably sad,
so forget everything I've said.

Cede

I think that we're no more than animal
and decorate ourselves with law and love,
with things that make us human— still we crawl,
but laws kill, and love likewise. Droves
of pretty feather, hoof and better hair
can have the earth. Eventually the air
will cleanly flow again, but not until
our breaths are wiped away to save it all.

I wish that gods were real enough and knew
a way to make us leave and take our souls—
the consciences we dug into the holes,
grabbing shiny things we thought we wanted.
I thought that language made us smart and true—
it only made us arrogant and stunted.
Let's walk all fours, chew the globe and moo
as beasts more human stand and learn to rule.

Out Damn Spot

Pour the wine down the drain,
it spills on your best clothes
and leaves an awful stain,

and you don't want to buy clothes again.
Your obvious choice,
to pour everything down the drain,

including poems that portray you vain,
and unrefrigerated groceries so close
to toxic you threw up and left your shirt stained,

so you went out and stood in the rain,
and for an hour you chose
to stand there, hoping to dissolve down the drain,

but you remained. Who's to blame
that you self-medicate and live a life loose,
but with a high-strung heart, and abstain

from acts that seem wrong. You can't explain
your complicated desires, and suppose
eventually you'll pour the wine down the drain,
though some things leave more awful stains.

The Penniless Speaks

It's not the world
that weights you while you mold
and mope,
but deficit of hope
for that comfortable pearl
sometimes deviously earned
by saps born blooming,
or gilded and booming,
and you weren't.

Eyeing the heap
of leching ordinaries
and turbo success stories,
today you're sad, and crumb
for a little glory,
a lucky leap.

Designated dumb,
you accept your minimal drive
and soar to the bottom.
We dive
only to rise, and thrive—
whatever.

Altitude is never
a factor of worth, and strata
are kept in check by some
who need a

monetary sense of momentum,
who don't confess
the sobering horror
of wealth's temporariness.

Rebel Lamb

People have their magic, then they die—
whims so full of promise and color—
things they believe and don't ask why.

I admit I have the urge to play
with faith for a life felt and fuller
before this thing around me starts to die—

the flesh, that is, gone dry
around the amassed soul or
this wad of electrical memories. Why

does it become a thing that supposedly flies
to a far *better* place where
those who died never die?

Is it ever too late to not believe, or try
to find living's earthly purpose, or another
who also believes in asking why

to the earth and that impossible sky?
We should fear afterlife, its chance of horror,
but people have their magic, then they die—
things they believe and don't ask why.

White Flag

Love with you must be surrender.
Don't leave us asunder.
I hand over my flow, my beat, the darts
of want that zero in to heart.

My parts
bind to you, to your dark matter,
to your whole wherever it wanders.

Turn, stoop, and carry me under
the stillest water
where lover leads lover to fondle
in a bed of iron trust, candlelight and bundle.

Prime Rib

He wants to carve out a piece of flesh, throw it on the wall,
or does he wish
he were all

the way dead? He's full
of crusted remorse, feeling so selfish
he'll run his head into a wall.

He feels small,
a speck, a dot of random flesh
who wants all

ache to end, who wants to pull
all the world to him, not push
it away anymore. *Carve out a piece of flesh for the wall,*

yeah tack it there, he thinks, *I was here— a tool,*
a dumb fish
who wanted all

but somehow dropped the ball.
He had such potential, and so much panache
they can paste his minnow skull to the wall
with heads of other fallen prey, revered by all.

Vulgarity Virgin

I don't use swear words,
even when I'm really miffed, I think
cursing's for the birds.

It doesn't sound sweet, I've heard
the worst from seedy people who stink,
so I don't use sewer words—

that would be like speaking in turds
instead of tongues, phrases so rank.
Cursing's for the birds—

not literally, they can't converse.
When I talked bad I got a good spank,
so I don't. Use swear words

in another, tawdrier universe
where even the pope is a filthy fink
cursing at the courtyard birds,

surely a place without the ear of God,
without one Christian soul to thank.
I don't use swear words—
cursing's for the birds.

The Dig

They'll excavate your brain to feel its weight
and stick electrodes in, from rot it will
renew. These resurrectionists await
enlightenment extracted from your noble

mush. Your genius, an arsenal
of truth, will be their prize, assuming any
ray from that abyss will make them feel
closer to your skewed view. You're weary

from thinking down and deep, but now at ease
as their appointed Sufferer With Class,
requiring grand homage, a martyr?— please!
So full of it. They should kick your ass

and bury you back beneath the bull, too prone
to claim your dumb mistakes were not your own.

the beast

out of the egg
of molestation
I rise
my dragon tails drag
I am wise

I am a mountain erection
rape is a violent meditation
I am an incest flower
with mama-sister's screaming eyes

I grow I spew I seek election
I 'm a ball of proud imperfection
lick brains— each head more power

the night is a baby that requires slapping
I dance into the dawn with a chainsaw
hacking and clapping
under-bed ghouls bowing
with squishy applause

I claw at family-friendly movies
fart infomercials
and steal into hospitals
collecting ovaries
to sell on sale
I crash C-section deliveries
to dowse with dirt the babies

I celebrate the rancid of my liver
I have lycan ears
suck down my tears
making the moon shiver
and abortions quiver

the hurricane of lost sperm churned
as I ate my father
and screwed my mother

into the valley of sick I plunge
my heart a numb sponge
I swim siphon the sewer
scissor-kick all that is pure
lonely women I lure
it's their flesh I need
every second I must feed
craving them to bleed
I will not die once you cut me
plead to me scare me
beware me

this is not your realness anymore
and I am keeping score
I have always been ahead
a head that rears itself to sin
the angels that defend you are dead

I want in you will peel your skin
bar the door
I'll get in
feel my stench blow
and know what I know
the sky will fall
I eat all

Sanctuary

Sanctum sanctorum,
may I come in,

seek refuge from the evil
that made my soul cave in?

There's trouble in
my chest, I'll stay a while

but far from the vestibule—
too near the monstrous wild.

If you require belief,
I'll feign and follow that rule

but never completely turn a leaf
even when cut with grief.

Preserve my naive child,
those remnants left in me.

Remove the filth, the paws
of my father on my skin—

an easy lair he hid in.
Is your savior really mild?

Who is on that cross?
Was he also defiled?

Forgive that I was touched.
He sinned so much.

The Lord, The Devil, The Dead

The lord, the devil, the dead— the in-between
I know so well, the first two don't exist,
and dead is one dead end, it's rarely known
what's here is all there is, but many risk

ignorance to think there's something more
deific to our birth and destination.
There's something in my common sense that stirs,
that says my soul's a lie of my creation

packed into a brain that's still so blind
and knows so little of what exists in full—
our desperation makes a soul to find,
and we make things to comfort us and pull

us into bliss— like gods are here unseen,
and we are more than cognizant machines.

www.ingramcontent.com/pod-product-compliance
Lightning Source LLC
Chambersburg PA
CBHW050023170726
48282CB00025B/520